GEORGE JOHNSON IS A SON-OF-A-BITCH

1st Edition, April, 1972
4th Printing, September, 1976

THE VALEDICTORIAN

1st Edition, September, 1976

THE HORTICULTURIST

1st Edition, September, 1976

ISBN 0-88754-040-6

PS
8587
M45
G4
1976

Smiley, Charles W., 1938-
  George Johnson is an S.O.B. ; The valedictorian ;
The horticulturist

ISBN 0-88754-040-6 pa.

I. Title.   II. Title: The valedictorian.
III. Title: The horticulturist.

PS8587.M45G4 1976   C812'.5'4   C76-017185-8
PR9199.3.S55G46 1976

GEORGE JOHNSON IS A SON-OF-A-BITCH

CHARACTERS:

GEORGE JOHNSON, a high-school teacher

MARIANNA HILL, a student

HELMUT SCHAFFER, a high-school teacher

George Johnson Is A Son-Of-A-Bitch was first produced
at the Factory Theatre Lab, Toronto, June 1972

> The scene opens to reveal a class-
> room. GEORGE JOHNSON, a teacher,
> is preparing to leave. A student
> enters.

MARIANNA: Excuse me.

GEORGE: Yes?

MARIANNA: Mr. Johnson?

GEORGE: Yes.

MARIANNA: I came in this morning. (Pause) Before school, remember?
You said to come back after school.

GEORGE: What do you want?

MARIANNA: I'd like to change into your third period class.

GEORGE: Interesting. Why is that?

MARIANNA: Why?

GEORGE: Yes. Why did you pick my class and why now?

MARIANNA: What do you mean?

GEORGE: Why not change at the semester break?

MARIANNA: (Pause) Can I change?

GEORGE: I don't have the power to change your programme. Counsel-
lors do that. Have you seen your counsellor?
      (MARIANNA starts to leave)
I can recommend a change. But I have to give a reason for
the change.

MARIANNA: Practical or emotional?

GEORGE: Either one.

MARIANNA: I have the same teacher I had last year. He's covering the
same material with the same old tired jokes. I'm not learn-
ing anything new.

GEORGE: Impossible. It's a different subject.

MARIANNA: Would you like to sit through two years of Mr. Schaffer?

GEORGE: What did you say your name was?

MARIANNA: Marianna... Marianna Hill.

GEORGE: How do you know I'll be any better than Mr. Schaffer?

MARIANNA: I don't know.

GEORGE: Why change to me then?

MARIANNA: I don't know.

GEORGE: Is there any other reason for the change?

MARIANNA: (She pulls a note out of her purse and reads it)
            "Will you please allow MARIANNA HILL to switch into your
            third period class?" Signed, "Helmut Schaffer".
                (She drops the note on GEORGE'S desk)
            He wants me out of his class.

GEORGE: Why didn't you tell me this earlier?

MARIANNA: I wanted to find out about you. I want to enter a class
            where I'm wanted.

GEORGE: Why does Mr. Schaffer want you out?

MARIANNA: Because I won't make love to him.

GEORGE: Well, if you won't make love to me, I don't want you in my
            class either. What do you have against making love?

MARIANNA: (She points to his cluttered desk)
            On a messy desk top like that?

GEORGE: (He laughs) It is rather sloppy isn't it?

MARIANNA: I didn't believe it.

GEORGE: About Mr. Schaffer? He would clean off his desk if you
            asked him.

MARIANNA: No, I mean you. The kids told me you played along. You do.
            (Pause) You know you have quite a reputation.

GEORGE: We all do. I work on several.

MARIANNA: I mean as a teacher.

GEORGE: I have several there too. Which one are you talking about?

MARIANNA: You don't provoke.

GEORGE: I don't what?

MARIANNA: Provoke. You don't provoke.

GEORGE: Is that good or bad?

MARIANNA: I'm not sure, but it's true.

GEORGE: Is that why you want to change into my class? To test my lack of provocation?

MARIANNA: No.

GEORGE: I might provoke you.

MARIANNA: I doubt it. Incidentally, your desk top is a mess.

GEORGE: I'll see what I can do to improve.

MARIANNA: You should.

GEORGE: I'll try to have you changed to my class.

MARIANNA: Thank you. (Pause. She looks around) This room looks like a lavatory. Not all your students like you, you know. I've heard them say, "Johnson is a cow".

GEORGE: My favourite is, "George Johnson is a mean son-of-a-bitch".

MARIANNA: Do you care?

GEORGE: About being called names or the messy classroom?

MARIANNA: No, I mean about my change of classes.

GEORGE: Your reasons are good enough. We're here to serve the students. Besides, if Mr. Schaffer wants you out, then...

MARIANNA: Teachers can have any student thrown out, right?

GEORGE: I doubt it. Why does Mr. Schaffer want you out?

MARIANNA: Ask him. I don't know.

GEORGE: Are you a good student?

MARIANNA: Why don't you check my record?

GEORGE: I sense provoking here.

MARIANNA: I'm only a student.

GEORGE: I believe in students.

MARIANNA: I get lousy grades.

GEORGE: What about in Mr. Schaffer's class?

MARIANNA: I'm flunking.

GEORGE: The hell you are. You can't change classes when you're failing. You know that.

MARIANNA: So forget it.

GEORGE: You aren't failing.

MARIANNA: You believe in students.

GEORGE: You aren't flunking.

MARIANNA: I'm lying.

GEORGE: It's more subtle than a lie.

MARIANNA: I'm flunking. Check my grades.

GEORGE: I'll be right back.

MARIANNA: Where are you going?

GEORGE: To look up your record in the office.
> (GEORGE exits. MARIANNA walks over to the blackboard and writes, "GEORGE JOHNSON IS A SON-OF-A BITCH". Then she looks through his desk, his grade book, and his papers. She opens a window, looks down, leaves the window open and hides in the room. GEORGE returns, sees the open window, looks down and closes the window. He sees her purse and picks it up)

All right, I'm curious. What's in here.
> (He empties the purse onto his desk)

Let's check. One key, one stick of gum, one pack of cigarettes, almost empty. One pack of matches, almost empty. One nickel. One pen. One dollar. Oh, yes, one aspirin. That's all. One normal female survival kit. Let's check the other record.
> (He reads from MARIANNA'S record)

Marianna Hill... I.Q. very high, classroom performance high, general aptitude high; grades last year... two A's, including Mr. Schaffer's class and four B's.

MARIANNA: (She comes out of hiding)
You aren't supposed to read the official record to the students.

GEORGE: I was provoked into it. You said you were failing Mr. Schaffer's class.

MARIANNA: To me I am.

GEORGE: (He looks at the record again)
            To me an A is not failing.

MARIANNA: What is more important, the grade or how you feel?

GEORGE: (He puts the record down. He turns and
            looks at the board)
            Your printing is terrible.

MARIANNA: The message is more important than the printing.

GEORGE: Who is your counsellor, Marianna? I'll write him a note that
          it's all right for you to change at the semester break. Third
          period isn't it?

MARIANNA: I don't care.

GEORGE: I think third period would be the easiest.

MARIANNA: I mean forget it.

GEORGE: You mean forget the change?

MARIANNA: Yes.

GEORGE: (He picks up the record book)
            Is the record accurate?

MARIANNA: What difference does it make?

GEORGE: You're after something. It doesn't show in here.

MARIANNA: Did you expect it to?

GEORGE: You mean the record is incomplete.

MARIANNA: The record is one-sided. There is only the shooting of the
          bloody teachers.

GEORGE: How many teachers have you shot down?

MARIANNA: My share. We students try to divide them up evenly.

GEORGE: Perhaps I will be more of a challenge for you.

MARIANNA: Can I see my record.
            (GEORGE gives her the record and begins
            to write a note for her counsellor)
          What would the principal do if he saw me reading this? What
          if I tear it up?

GEORGE: It's not yours to destroy.

MARIANNA: It has my name on it, Marianna Hill. I am Marianna Hill.

GEORGE: I know, flesh and blood and feelings and all that.

MARIANNA: Did you ever see yours?

GEORGE: See my what?

MARIANNA: Your official school record, silly.

GEORGE: No. I never found out what I was really like.
                    (GEORGE holds out his hand. MARIANNA
                    gives back her record)
                I'll take it back to the office. I wrote a note to your coun-
                sellor about the class change. Should I give it to him?

MARIANNA: No. I can't decide.

GEORGE: If Mr. Schaffer wants you out...

MARIANNA: I might not want to change to you.
                    (She holds out her hand. GEORGE gives
                    her the note)

GEORGE: I'll be right back.
                    (GEORGE exits. MARIANNA reads the note
                    and drops it on GEORGE'S desk. She writes
                    on the board, under her first message,
                    "AND HE TRIES TOO HARD". Then she picks
                    up his grade book and thumbs through it.
                    GEORGE re-enters)

MARIANNA: You don't put many marks in your grade books.

GEORGE: Just enough to keep everybody happy.

MARIANNA: Do you like teaching?

GEORGE: Out there.
                    (He gestures to the room. He gestures
                    to the gradebook, and then looks at the
                    blackboard)
                You aren't supposed to show the official record to the tea-
                chers.

MARIANNA: Don't erase it.

GEORGE: Why not?

MARIANNA: It's not yours to erase.

GEORGE: Have you decided about the class change?

MARIANNA: No.

GEORGE: Look, Marianna, keep the note. Use it if you want. I sense you are here for something else, but this guessing game could go on all night. (Pause) Is there anything else? I don't know you, Marianna.

MARIANNA: You read my official record.

GEORGE: I still don't know you.

MARIANNA: Go home then.

GEORGE: What is it?

MARIANNA: Questions from a teacher; to hear answers they already know.

GEORGE: I don't play games, Marianna.

MARIANNA: But, I do.

GEORGE: All right.

MARIANNA: What do you think my problem is?

GEORGE: I don't know.

MARIANNA: Aren't you interested in my problem?

GEORGE: I don't think you know what it is?

MARIANNA: Take a guess.

GEORGE: You're looking for sex that you can justify as love.
            (There is a long pause)

MARIANNA: I know what my problem is. The question we are facing is, why do you want to know?

GEORGE: I have to know... first.

MARIANNA: Before you can help me?

GEORGE: Yes.

MARIANNA: Why should you help me?

GEORGE: Maybe I won't help you. Maybe I can't.

MARIANNA: Why are you here?

GEORGE: Here, now?

MARIANNA: Why are you a teacher here?

GEORGE: It's not why. It's how.

MARIANNA: All right. How are you here.

GEORGE: As myself.

MARIANNA: Bullshit.
          (GEORGE does not react. MARIANNA holds
          up his grade book)

GEORGE: I compromise to stay here.

MARIANNA: Then you'll compromise with me.

GEORGE: How?

MARIANNA: To stay here, you have to keep me as a student and you must
          be the teacher. You can't let me be Marianna Hill, and you
          can't be yourself.

GEORGE: Bullshit.
          (MARIANNA does react. She is taken aback)

MARIANNA: The problem is, Mr. Schaffer.

GEORGE: What is it?

MARIANNA: Ask him.

GEORGE: Ask him what?

MARIANNA: So go home then.

GEORGE: You really need these games don't you. All right, I am the
          teacher here. So you can go home, Marianna Hill.

MARIANNA: Mr. Schaffer wants me.

GEORGE: You mean sexually?

MARIANNA: He wants me.

GEORGE: You're wrong.

MARIANNA: The note is a fake. I wrote it myself.
          (GEORGE walks to the wall phone, picks
          it up and...)

GEORGE: Mr. Schaffer's room, please. Hello, Helmut. This is George
          Johnson. Are you busy? Oh, yeah. Well, could you stop
          by my room for a minute on your way out? Good. 106.

(GEORGE hangs up the phone)

MARIANNA: What are you going to do?

GEORGE: Talk to Mr. Schaffer about you.

MARIANNA: Oh.

GEORGE: You better go.

MARIANNA: Why?

GEORGE: Do you want to stay?

MARIANNA: No.

> (MARIANNA exits. GEORGE reads the note
> from MR. SCHAFFER again. He starts to
> erase the blackboard, but decides not
> to. HELMUT SCHAFFER enters)

HELMUT: Hi. Everyday I haul home more and more crap.

GEORGE: I would think a veteran like you would have a system to beat the paperwork.

HELMUT: I do. I just haul it back and forth and never touch it. What's the problem? About the faculty talent show?

GEORGE: No, something else.

HELMUT: God. You know, I used to teach in this room. I hated it. Hot. Hell, all the kids needed showers after an hour in here. This room was handcrafted for educational fatigue.

GEORGE: It hasn't been too bad.

HELMUT: Wait until winter. Do you know the floor shakes when the furnace comes one? It's right below here.

GEORGE: At least it's the ground floor. We make it out first if there's a fire.

HELMUT: Hell, if there's a fire, nobody gets out. Do you know this dungeon has a wooden roof? Yeah, wooden beams, the whole bit. God damn, I remember this room.

GEORGE: What kind of student is Marianna Hill?

HELMUT: Damn good. Why.

GEORGE: She asked me if she could change into my third period class.

HELMUT: That's funny. I wonder why?

GEORGE: You don't want her out?

HELMUT: Hell no. Marianna Hill is a cute girl. Did she give a reason?

GEORGE: She just said she wants to change. Any reason you can think of?

HELMUT: No, I had her last year. She'll get an A from me. Damn nice girl.

GEORGE: She is pretty.

HELMUT: Hell, yes.

GEORGE: Is she popular?

HELMUT: I don't know. She didn't tell you her problem, huh?

GEORGE: No.

HELMUT: She has been bitchy lately. Maybe she was screwed by one of the boys.

GEORGE: Think so?

HELMUT: I don't know. She wears some kind of love button all the time. Free love, I think. (Pause) She would be a nice piece to get free. (Pause) She hasn't worn the button for the last two days. I'll have to ask her what her price is now.

GEORGE: About the class change...

HELMUT: I'll ask her tomorrow. She's probably just sick of me.

GEORGE: Could be.

HELMUT: I've had her two years. (Pause) Is that all?

GEORGE: Yes, I was just curious.

HELMUT: If she wants to change, it's all right with me. If she does, put her in the front row. Department meeting tomorrow, right?

GEORGE: Right.

HELMUT: See you later.

GEORGE: Right.

HELMUT: Remember, it's not an earthquake. It's just the furnace.

(MR. SCHAFFER exits. GEORGE prepares to leave, but MARIANNA comes back into the classroom)

MARIANNA: Well, what happened?

GEORGE: He said you could change.

MARIANNA: I know. I was listening outside the door.

GEORGE: I thought you would.

MARIANNA: (She mimics GEORGE) I thought you would. Don't you trust me?

GEORGE: I'm not sure.

MARIANNA: Remember, you believe in students.

GEORGE: Why do you want to change?

MARIANNA: He wants me.

GEORGE: All right. You look desirable. But, has he ever tried to get you?

MARIANNA: No.

GEORGE: You have been lying to me.

MARIANNA: Yes. Are you provoked?

GEORGE: I'm going home.

MARIANNA: If I went to the office and told them, what would happen?

GEORGE: It would be your word against his.

MARIANNA: Would he be fired?

GEORGE: I doubt it.

MARIANNA: Why?

GEORGE: You have no proof. He has a good record.

MARIANNA: My record is good.

GEORGE: You are a student.

MARIANNA: The truth is... he thinks of me as a nice piece of ass. Why doesn't he write that in my official record?

GEORGE: Is that what you want to be remembered as, a nice piece of ass?

MARIANNA: What do you write about your students?

GEORGE: As little as possible.

MARIANNA: Why?

GEORGE: I talk to my students.

MARIANNA: Oh, I see. George Johnson gives it directly to the students. An open file.

GEORGE: Something like that.

MARIANNA: How far will you go.
(MARIANNA tips over a desk)

GEORGE: What are you doing?

MARIANNA: Don't move or I'll scream.
(She tips over another desk)
I'm going to the office. It will be my official record against yours.

GEORGE: Why me?

MARIANNA: You're here and you deserve it.
(She knocks the papers and books off his desk)

GEORGE: Why do I deserve it?

MARIANNA: You have molested me. You felt my breasts.

GEORGE: How bizarre. Why would I do that?

MARIANNA: Why doesn't matter. It's how and you did it.

GEORGE: I won't lose my job.

MARIANNA: They'll think I'm telling the truth.

GEORGE: You should always be honest.
(GEORGE slowly walks over to MARIANNA, and very deliberately squeezes both her breasts. MARIANNA does not react)
Now go to the office.
(GEORGE begins picking up the desks. MARIANNA writes on the blackboard, "HE IS EASILY PROVOKED". She turns)

MARIANNA: I'll see my counsellor tomorrow about the class change.
(MARIANNA exits. GEORGE prepares to
leave, starts to erase the blackboard,
decides not to, and then exits)

THE END

THE VALEDICTORIAN

CHARACTERS:

CHRISTINE

DAVE

A MAN

The Valedictorian was first produced at the Bakersfield
Community College, Bakersfield, California, November
1971

THE VALEDICTORIAN

Scene: the mens' room in a Grey-
hound Bus station. It is late in
the evening. CHRISTINE, an attrac-
tive young girl, is huddled, trem-
bling, under one of the sinks.
DAVE, a young man, walks into the
restroom.

DAVE: Oh... (He is embarrassed) Excuse me. I thought...
                 (He backs out of the door. There is
                 a slight pause and then he comes back)
             Pardon me, but this is the right place for me.
                 (He waits for a response. There is none)
             For me I mean. (Still no response) If you work here I
             uh... well, I would feel more comfortable if you would
             wait outside for a few minutes.
                 (Still no response. He turns around
                 and leaves. After another short pause
                 he comes back)
             Lady, this is the mens' restroom.

CHRISTINE: (Timidly) I know.

DAVE: Well... uh... (He gestures toward the door) Shouldn't
             you leave?

CHRISTINE: (She rises and walks toward the door, but
                 freezes halfway there)
             I can't.

DAVE: What?

CHRISTINE: I can't go.

DAVE: You can't go where?

CHRISTINE: Out into the lobby.

DAVE: What are you talking about?

CHRISTINE: There are so many people out there. They'll see me when
             I leave and laugh at me. Some of them are probably riding
             on my bus. Don't you see? I can't go out there now.

DAVE: Well... listen, Miss, or whoever you are. I've a long bus
             ride, and I have to go. (CHRISTINE remains frozen)
             So, if you don't mind!

CHRISTINE: (She bursts into tears) I tried, but I can't make myself.
I'm supposed to be the example. I'm the one everyone is
supposed to look up to, and here I am in this place. I was
Valedictorian of my class.

DAVE: What is this? Am I on Candid Camera?
    (CHRISTINE starts crying again and runs
    back under the sink)
Now, don't cry. (He looks nervously at the door) Someone
is going to think I hit you or... something worse. Please,
Miss, stop. I'm not going to do anything. Just tell me
what you want.

CHRISTINE: I was Valedictorian of my class.

DAVE: What the hell does that have to do with anything?

CHRISTINE: (Another tearful outburst) People are supposed to look up
to me.

DAVE: They can't do it with you in your present position. Will
you come out of there? You look like a scared mole.
(CHRISTINE starts to come out) What am I doing? (CHRIS-
TINE withdraws again) What the hell is going on? I can't
be messed up in this. I have a bus to catch and it's a
long ride, and... damnit, I have to use the head, I mean
lavatory. So, you can stay or leave. I don't care.
    (He waits for CHRISTINE to leave. She
    doesn't move)
All right. You've had your chance.
    (DAVE begins to walk toward the urinal,
    reaching for his zipper. CHRISTINE screams)
Jesus Christ, lady. What are you trying to do? If you
want to get out of here, go. I'm not keeping you. (Pause)
Are you going to leave? (CHRISTINE doesn't move) Will you
please leave. I'll hold the door for you. (Still no res-
ponse) Well then, will you sit there quietly? You can
look the other way and cover your ears.
    (Still no response. He backs toward the
    urinal)
I know this is awkward and embarrassing for you, but think
how it is for me. You know how it is when nature calls
... after a while she really calls.
    (DAVE laughs nervously. CHRISTINE doesn't
    respond. She stares into space. DAVE turns
    quickly toward the urinal and reaches for his
    zipper. CHRISTINE screams)
The hell with it! I'll bust a kidney.
    (He begins to walk toward the door)
(Muttering) I've seen some nutty broads before, but
you're one...

CHRISTINE: (She stands up) Don't leave. Help me.
(DAVE stops, turns back and then starts
to leave again)
Please. (DAVE stops) Help me.

DAVE: (He turns back to CHRISTINE) Help you with what?

CHRISTINE: Help me to get out.

DAVE: Are you sick?

CHRISTINE: No.

DAVE: Then what's wrong?

CHRISTINE: I can't leave.

DAVE: Is this a joke? I mean, all you have to do is walk out the
door.

CHRISTINE: You don't understand.

DAVE: An understatement if ever I heard one.

CHRISTINE: All the people out there would see me coming out.

DAVE: They might.

CHRISTINE: This is the men's restroom.

DAVE: I'm beginning to wonder. I thought it was a new kind of
sit-in demonstration. (CHRISTINE begins crying) Don't
start crying. Relax. I'm not sure what the problem is,
or how you expect me to help you, but it seems to me you
only have to walk out the door. No one is going to notice.
Most of the people are loading on their buses now, anyway.
Stand up and leave. There's really no problem.

CHRISTINE: Not all of them.

DAVE: Not all of them what?

CHRISTINE: Not all the people are loading. Some of them will see me.
I don't know what to do. I didn't know it was the men's
restroom. I'm not the kind of girl who goes into a place
like this. I'm a nice girl, and if anyone should see me
coming out and tell my mother and friends, I'd just die.

DAVE: You can't walk out?

CHRISTINE: No.

DAVE: What if you hid behind me as I walked out?

CHRISTINE: No. It would look even worse.

DAVE: I guess it would.
            (He starts backing toward the entrance
            door)
            Well listen. I would like to help. I've always wanted to
            be a social worker, but I do have to go... er, leave. You
            have to find the guts to walk out. That's all I can tell
            you.
            (DAVE turns to walk out the door, but
            CHRISTINE runs toward him, falls at his
            feet and grabs him around the knees)

CHRISTINE: Oh, please. Please don't leave me. You have to help me.

DAVE: (Extremely shaken) For Christ's sake lady! You made an
            honest mistake. Now you're making a major production out
            of it. (He struggles to get away) Will you let go of my
            legs. Please. Before someone comes in. (There is a short
            pause) If a man should walk in here with you like this,
            then you would have something to be embarrassed about.
            (CHRISTINE, moved by this logic, quiets
            her tears and rises to her feet)
            O.K. You're doing better. All right, suppose I did help
            you, just pretend, what would you want me to do?

CHRISTINE: I don't know.

DAVE: You don't know?

CHRISTINE: No.

DAVE: Well then, let's think this whole problem through from the
            beginning. (He assumes the role of a thinker) Your basic
            problem is, you want to leave the men's restroom of the
            Greyhound Bus station, so to speak? But you are afraid the
            people in the lobby will see you coming out of the men's
            restroom and laugh at you. Is that a correct analysis of
            the problem?

CHRISTINE: Yes. You're very intelligent.

DAVE: Well, thank you. (Pause) Let's see, if you had just peeked
            your head in and had not come all the way in on your ini-
            tial entrance, and had then backed right out, you wouldn't
            have this problem now. True?

CHRISTINE: I... I guess so.

DAVE: Your problem is solved. All you have to do is walk out and look a little startled, you know, as if you had just walked in and walked right back out. No one's going to know you've been in here for a few minutes. Isn't it simple?
(DAVE smiles and hopes she will accept the idea)

CHRISTINE: You don't understand. I've been in here for an hour and a half.

DAVE: You've what?

CHRISTINE: I've been here for an hour and a half.

DAVE: But how...? Why in the hell have you stayed in here that long?

CHRISTINE: I had to.

DAVE: Why?

CHRISTINE: Well... because.

DAVE: Why because?

CHRISTINE: Because... I came in, and I didn't notice I was in the wrong restroom so I... Oh, I just can't.
(CHRISTINE runs and hides under the sink again)

DAVE: Now, control yourself. You have to tell me what happened if I'm going to help you.

CHRISTINE: I... well, I...

DAVE: Tell me.

CHRISTINE: (She blurts out) I went to the bathroom.

DAVE: (He starts laughing) But how in the world...? Didn't you notice the difference?
(DAVE points to the urinals)

CHRISTINE: (She shrieks out) No, I didn't. I didn't see them.

DAVE: Then how did you find out?

CHRISTINE: I saw the writing on the walls.

DAVE: You mean...? (He points to one of the stalls and laughs harder) That's very funny.

CHRISTINE: (She begins to cry) Oh yes, that's very funny.

DAVE: (He stops laughing) Well you see, you said you saw the
             writing on the wall. It's just like... please, don't start
             crying again. I'm sorry. I didn't mean to upset you.
                  (DAVE moves toward her)

CHRISTINE: Stay away. I don't want you to help me now.

DAVE: What?

CHRISTINE: Get away.

DAVE: But I thought... What did I do?

CHRISTINE: You think I'm so funny. Well, go ahead and laugh at me.
             It wouldn't be very funny if you were in a men's restroom.

DAVE: But, I am!

CHRISTINE: Well, women's restroom then. Go away.

DAVE: Listen, I'm sorry. I didn't mean to laugh. It's just...
             your situation is a little humorous.

CHRISTINE: You can go outside and laugh all you want. Leave me alone.

DAVE: No, I won't. I'm going to stay here and help. So, you
             can calm down. (Pause) Say, what about the wastebasket?

CHRISTINE: The wastebasket?

DAVE: Sure.
                  (He picks up the wastebasket and brings
                  it over to CHRISTINE)
             You could hide in here, and then I could drag it out as if
             I were going to empty it. When I got it outside to some-
             place where no one would see you, you could jump out.

CHRISTINE: Do you think it will work?

DAVE: Why not? It's worth a try.
                  (He dumps all the paper towels out of
                  the basket onto the floor)
             Here, climb in.
                  (CHRISTINE climbs into the basket)
             I don't know why I didn't think of this before. It's so
             easy. You'll have to crouch down. Maybe we'd better cover
             you.
                  (He begins throwing the paper towels
                  over CHRISTINE)

CHRISTINE: Are you sure it will work?

DAVE: Sure, I'm sure.

CHRISTINE: What if someone sees me?

DAVE: They can't see you under the paper towels.
                 (He finishes covering her. He is excited
                 over the adventure)
            Are you ready for the big break?

CHRISTINE: Ready.

DAVE: Brace yourself inside so you won't be bounced around.

CHRISTINE: All right.

DAVE: O.K. Here we go.
                 (DAVE makes an attempt to move the basket,
                 but the added weight has made it too heavy.
                 He tries several times, becoming more and
                 more frustrated. Finally in a last surge
                 of strength he pulls the basket, and CHRIS-
                 TINE, down on top of himself)

CHRISTINE: Am I out?

DAVE: No, you're not out!
                 (CHRISTINE climbs out of the basket and
                 looks around)

CHRISTINE: What happened? Is someone outside the door?

DAVE: (He is irritated) There's no one outside.

CHRISTINE: Then how come we're not going?

DAVE: Because of my back. I forgot about my bad back. I'm not
            supposed to do any strenuous work.

CHRISTINE: I see.

DAVE: Doctor's orders.

CHRISTINE: Oh... Thank you for trying. It's very kind of you, and
            more than most people would do.

DAVE: My damn back.

CHRISTINE: Don't blame yourself. It's not your fault.

DAVE: It could have worked.

CHRISTINE: I guess I'm too heavy. I should go on a diet. (Fishing for a compliment) How could you move someone as fat as me?

DAVE: Damn back.

CHRISTINE: I'm just too fat.

DAVE: Huh?

CHRISTINE: I said you couldn't be expected to move me. I'm overweight.

DAVE: Oh, no. No. It's not true at all. You look very, well... pretty.

CHRISTINE: Oh, I do not.

DAVE: Yes, you do.

CHRISTINE: Really?

DAVE: Absolutely.

CHRISTINE: Well, thank you. No one has ever told me before.

DAVE: I don't believe you.

CHRISTINE: It's true.

DAVE: (He is embarrassed) Maybe we'd better pick up the towels.
(They begin to pick up the paper towels
and place them in the basket)
What's your name?

CHRISTINE: Christine; my friends call me Christy.

DAVE: Hey, the same as my mother's name.

CHRISTINE: It is?

DAVE: Yes, Christine... Christine. She was a prostitute.

CHRISTINE: Your mother?

DAVE: No. I mean in the Bible. Christine. She was a prostitute. She slept with a king or something.

CHRISTINE: I'm sorry. I didn't mean to say...

DAVE: It's all right. I guess I wasn't too clear. My name's Dave.

CHRISTINE: Hello, Dave.

DAVE: Hello, Christine... er, Christy. You know, I read in a
           book once about a celebrity who was in a situation like
           this.

CHRISTINE: You did?

DAVE: Yes. It seemed this man was at a theatre and he acci-
           dentally walked into the wrong room, and before he knew
           it a group of women started to walk in too. So (He be-
           gins to laugh), he quickly pulled a lighter out of his pock-
           et, lit it and stood there like the Statue of Liberty.
           When one woman screamed and asked him what he was doing,
           he told her he worked there; it was a little extra service
           provided by the management. He was the official seat
           warmer. (They both laugh) Say, didn't anyone else come
           in while you were here.

CHRISTINE: There weren't any buses leaving or arriving until now. I
           guess there haven't been many people here tonight.

DAVE: It is late. You've been pretty lucky.

CHRISTINE: I know.

DAVE: That's one blessing you can count. (Laughs nervously)

CHRISTINE: What?

DAVE: Blessing you can count. You know, "count your blessings".

CHRISTINE: Oh... How did he get out?

DAVE: Who?

CHRISTINE: The man in the book.

DAVE: Oh, him. He asked the lady what time it was and when she
           told him he said, "Oh my God. It's five minutes past quit-
           ting time" and then he walked out.

CHRISTINE: Oh.

DAVE: I was going to San Francisco. Where were you headed?

CHRISTINE: Reno.

DAVE: Reno's a nice city. I've always liked Reno. Did you know
           in the bus depot there they have attendants in the men's
           rooms? Guys who shine your shoes and sell you papers and
           stuff? I guess you couldn't get stuck in there, could you?

DAVE:
(CHRISTINE becomes agitated)
(Cont'd) I'm sorry. I guess this isn't the best topic of conversation, is it? Well, don't worry, I'll figure out a way....
(Footsteps are heard outside)
Someone is coming.

CHRISTINE: Oh, no. What am I going to do?

DAVE: I don't know.

CHRISTINE: I'll have to hide.
(CHRISTINE runs over and crouches under the sink)

DAVE: No. Not there. That's no good. Here. Go into one of the stalls.

CHRISTINE: I can't!

DAVE: Why not?

CHRISTINE: I don't have another nickel.

DAVE: (Digging into his pockets) Oh, hell, maybe I have one.
(He gives up the search) I don't have a nickel either.

CHRISTINE: What am I going to do?

DAVE: Crawl under the door.

CHRISTINE: I couldn't do that.

DAVE: Sure you could. There's plenty of room.

CHRISTINE: But it would be against the law.

DAVE: Cheat! No one's going to report you.
(He pushes CHRISTINE toward the stall)
Hurry!
(She slips under the door of the stall just as a MAN walks in. DAVE grabs and shakes the hand of the MAN who walked in)
Hello, my name is Dave.

THE MAN: (He mutters) Good evening.
(The MAN walks toward the stall where CHRISTINE is hiding. DAVE panics and shouts)

DAVE: No!

THE MAN: I beg your pardon.

DAVE: (He is embarrassed at his outburst) I... uh... I said...
             No.

THE MAN: I know what you said, but why did you say it?

DAVE: Well... you can't use the toilet.

THE MAN: And why not?

DAVE: Dysentery. There's a wild epidemic of dysentery in this
             neighborhood. I'm from the local health board. I was about
             to call and have signs placed in here to quarantine the
             restroom.

THE MAN: But I thought one received dysentery orally. From drink-
             ing or eating bad foods.

DAVE: Well, you can't eat or drink in here either.

THE MAN: What in heaven's name are you trying to tell me? Surely
             it's safe for me to use the lavatory as long as I refrain
             from touching the facilities?

DAVE: I wouldn't do it if I were you.

THE MAN: I'm afraid I have no other choice than to take the risk.
             It's out of my hands.
                   (The MAN crosses to the urinal. DAVE
                   rushes up)

DAVE: But this is a very strong, active germ. It will jump right
             up on you.

THE MAN: I'll stand six feet away.

DAVE: You braggart.

THE MAN: I don't know what this nonsense is, but if you don't let
             me pass I shall call the manager.
                   (The MAN breaks away and heads for the
                   stall again)

DAVE: Wait.
                   (He pulls an old, crumpled piece of
                   paper and pencil from his pocket)
             I'll have to ask you to sign this.

THE MAN: What is it?

DAVE: It's a release. It releases me from any responsibility over what might happen to you. Just sign here. It keeps me out of trouble with the Mayor.

THE MAN: The Mayor?

DAVE: Yes, sir.

THE MAN: Is this some kind of a joke? Am I on Candid Camera?
>   (The MAN starts looking around the walls
>   for a hidden camera)

DAVE: It's no joke.

THE MAN: We'll just have to find out. I'm going to see the manager about this. How would you like that?

DAVE: I wouldn't if I were you.

THE MAN: And why not?

DAVE: He has dysentery breath. I'm getting a sign for him, too.

THE MAN: This is the most ridiculous thing I've ever heard. We'll see about this.
>   (The MAN storms out of the door)

CHRISTINE: (From inside the stall) Is he gone?

DAVE: Yes. You can come out now.
>   (CHRISTINE crawls from underneath the
>   door. She removes one of her shoes and
>   proceeds to dump water out of it onto
>   the floor)
>   What happened?

CHRISTINE: I stood up on the... well, on the thing so he wouldn't see my legs and I slipped.

DAVE: Both feet?

CHRISTINE: No, just one.

DAVE: (He crosses and listens at the door) I think he's going to come back.

CHRISTINE: Couldn't we barricade the door?

DAVE: It's against the law. You'd be depriving man of one of his constitutional rights.

CHRISTINE: Oh... Thanks anyway for helping me.

DAVE: You don't have to thank me. It wasn't difficult.

CHRISTINE: You shouldn't belittle what you did. It was marvelous.
            You're very clever.

DAVE: It's practical application of high school debating.

CHRISTINE: You used to debate?

DAVE: Yes. Before I went into the service. I was just dis-
            charged. But listen, the man is coming back. We have to
            think of a way to get you out of here.
                 (There is a pause while he paces back
                 and forth, thinking)
            My jacket. You could wear my jacket. No one would notice
            you then. Here, put it on.
                 (He hands her the jacket and she puts
                 it on)
            It's a little big, but not everyone can have a tailored
            suit.
                 (The jacket hangs over her fingers
                 and looks somewhat like an overcoat,
                 much too large)

CHRISTINE: My skirt. (She notices it is exposed) It can be seen.

DAVE: Your skirt?

CHRISTINE: Below the jacket.

DAVE: Do you think anyone would notice?

CHRISTINE: It hangs down a long way.

DAVE: Maybe you could take it off.
                 (CHRISTINE gives him a shocked start)
            I'm sorry. I was trying to come up with a solution. You
            couldn't pose as a Scotsman, could you?
                 (CHRISTINE continues to stare at him)
            Just a thought.

CHRISTINE: I don't think the coat is going to work.

DAVE: What if I gave you my pants?

CHRISTINE: Your pants?

DAVE: Sure. I could slip into the booth and hand them out to
            you.

CHRISTINE: What would you wear?

DAVE: Oh... You're right. That would create another problem, wouldn't it.

CHRISTINE: If you gave me your pants and waited in there, I could leave and change, and then throw them back into you when I was ready.

DAVE: Say, that's not a bad idea. It would only take a couple of minutes. Sure, why not? Wait one second.
          (DAVE slides under the door of the stall
          and begins to take off his pants)

CHRISTINE: This is terribly kind of you. I hope I haven't made you late for San Francisco. I mean, I hope you don't have an appointment.

DAVE: No. There's plenty of time. I'm going there to find a job on a fishing boat.
          (DAVE hands out his pants. CHRISTINE
          slips out of her skirt and begins to
          put on his pants. She hangs her skirt
          over the wastebasket)

CHRISTINE: How exciting.

DAVE: I hope so. My family wants me to enter college. But, I don't want to go. College is a drag. Everyone goes now because it's the thing to do. What are you going to do in Reno?

CHRISTINE: Attend college at the University.

DAVE: I'm sorry. I didn't mean everyone in college...

CHRISTINE: I understand.

DAVE: You do?

CHRISTINE: Yes. I guess the only reason I'm going is because of my father's insurance policy.

DAVE: Insurance policy?

CHRISTINE: He bought one of those policies when I was born that gives your child enough money to attend college when old enough. It's the main reason I worked so hard to be Valedictorian. My father's been the happiest man in the world since graduation. And now I'm on my way to college, he's beside himself.

CHRISTINE: I've never danced like this in front of someone before.

DAVE: You should. You should belly dance all the time.

CHRISTINE: I'd like to.

DAVE: Then do it. The hell with your father.

CHRISTINE: But I...
             (CHRISTINE turns away from the stall to
             put on DAVE'S pants. DAVE has become
             excited about his idea and comes out of
             the stall. He is wearing only his shorts
             and socks)

DAVE: No, no buts. If you want to belly dance then why should
             you be forced to study physics and astronomy? The world
             needs belly dancers more than it needs scientists and social
             workers.

CHRISTINE: I have to graduate from college.

DAVE: No you don't. Be yourself.
             (CHRISTINE turns around, sees DAVE
             in his shorts, screams and then runs
             and hides under the sink)
             Oh, I'm sorry. I didn't....
             (He grabs her skirt from the wastebasket,
             backs into a corner and puts it on)
             I wasn't thinking. I'm sorry. You can come out now. I
             didn't mean to offend you.
             (CHRISTINE comes out from under the
             sink. She looks at DAVE and starts
             laughing)
             What are you laughing at? (He looks down at himself in
             the skirt) Well, it was the only thing around. It was
             right here.

CHRISTINE: I didn't mean to laugh.

DAVE: I must look pretty silly.

CHRISTINE: A little, but I shouldn't laugh. You're doing all this
             for me.

DAVE: We have to help each other.

CHRISTINE: How beautiful. I hope you're not upset by my laughing at
             you.

DAVE: Oh, no, no. I'm not upset.

CHRISTINE: Are you sure?

DAVE: I'm confused, is what I am. I came in here to take a...
             I mean, to use the bathroom, and then you... and now
             this. I don't know what I'm doing.

CHRISTINE: You're trying to help me.

DAVE: I must be out of my mind. Hell, I'm going to catch my
             bus.

CHRISTINE: Me too. I'll walk out with you.

DAVE: Come on then.
                  (They start to walk out of the rest-
                  room, but DAVE stops)
             Now wait, what is this? What am I doing? I can't go
             out like this.

CHRISTINE: Why not?

DAVE: I'm wearing a skirt. What are people going to think.
             All those people out there will laugh at me.

CHRISTINE: No one's going to notice. Most of the people are loading
             on their buses now, anyway.

DAVE: But, I'll be arrested.

CHRISTINE: No you won't. The people won't notice you. Be brave.
             We can walk outside and when we're alone we can change
             back.

DAVE: But I...

CHRISTINE: You're helping me. You're my hero.

DAVE: I'm crazy.
                  (CHRISTINE grabs his arm and they start
                  to walk toward the door. DAVE looks con-
                  fused. They hear footsteps outside)
             Oh, my God. Someone is coming.
                  (He begins to push CHRISTINE toward the
                  stalls)
             Quick, get back in there. I'll think of something.

CHRISTINE: Do you have a match?

DAVE: A match? At a time like this you need a cigarette?
             Hurry, crawl into the john.

CHRISTINE: I need a match.

DAVE: You're the nuttiest broad.
                   (He fumbles in his pocket and produces
                   a match book)
              Here. Now hurry, crawl under the...
                   (The MAN who has been in previously
                   comes in)

THE MAN: Now listen, I've seen the manager and he says he doesn't
              have dysentery breath.
                   (The MAN looks at CHRISTINE, who
                   calmly strikes a match, and poses
                   like the Statue of Liberty. The
                   MAN stares at her)
              What in the hell is going on in here?

CHRISTINE: It's a little extra service we offer, sir. I'm the official
              seat warmer.

THE MAN: The seat warmer!

CHRISTINE: Yes sir.
                   (CHRISTINE grabs DAVE by the arm
                   and begins to lead him out. She
                   looks back at the MAN)
              We hope you have a comfortable stay. The seat in the
              third stall has been warmed to exactly 72 degrees, sir.
                   (CHRISTINE and DAVE exit. The MAN
                   looks extremely confused)

THE END

THE HORTICULTURIST

CHARACTERS:

GEORGE JOHNSON

CARETAKER OF A PARK

DOROTHY, George's wife

MARICIA, George's daughter

The Horticulturist was first produced at the University of Missouri, Columbia, Missouri, February 1972

THE HORTICULTURIST

The play is set in a park. There is
a small garden of roses. It is late
afternoon. GEORGE JOHNSON enters
the stage carrying a manuscript and
an American flag. The flag is large
and is on a 6-foot pole. GEORGE
sticks the flag in the ground amidst
the roses. He addresses the audience.

GEORGE: The problem is with the time; with the age; with man in general and in specific. It is an experience associated with
the polar reaches of our vast wasteland. Ice. Ice will be
the downfall of the future generation, and with this specific
member of this generation in particular. For ice in cubes,
and in flakes, and in bergs has crept, or rather crysta-
lized, into the hearts of our women, that is to say our
wives. Frigidity is driving man to untold, to unspoken
degradation, degeneration, and decay. We cannot close our
eyes to the ice that is smothering our fertilic processes.
It is a known, scientific fact the sperm cell needs a cer-
tain degree of warmth to survive. Without this warmth the
cell dies and there is no reproduction. I ask you to think
about the significance of the statement. Without warmth
the sperm must die. With a dead sperm there can be no fertilization of the egg, and without a fertilization of the
egg there can be no babies. And a race without babies is
doomed to extinction. Have you ever asked yourself why
this country has the lowest birthrate in the world? This is
why I have come to speak to you today about man as a free
agent, in general, and my wife who is, frankly, a frigid
bitch, in specific. As I stand here before you we are
faced with what promises to become...
        (The CARETAKER of the park comes running
        on to the stage)

CARETAKER: Here now, be careful; you're in the roses.

GEORGE: ... the greatest Ice Age of them all.

CARETAKER: The roses. You're walking in the flowers. That's malici-
ous destruction of city property. You'll have to find some-
where else to make your speech. The rose bed is not a town
meeting hall.

GEORGE: Are you speaking to me?

CARETAKER: I certainly am.

GEORGE: I must ask you to hold your questions for the press confer-
              ence which will be held right after I've finished the speech.
              You've caused me to lose my train of thought.

CARETAKER: I'm not asking questions. I'm telling you to get out of
              the roses.

GEORGE: But, I'm making a speech.

CARETAKER: It makes no difference. If you can't orate without orating
              all over the roses, then you'll have to leave the park.
              I've been working on these roses for thirty-three years.
                   (GEORGE moves out of the roses)

GEORGE: Is this all right?

CARETAKER: Oh, you're all right there, but that's not the point. I've
              been working on these roses for thirty-three years and
              you've trampled all over them. Hybrids, too. Artificially
              inseminated by my own hand. And believe me, it's not an
              easy job.

GEORGE: Artificially inseminated? Flowers?

CARETAKER: I've been studying it for years.   The bees have become
              lazy. They don't do a proper job any more. So, I have to
              put a hand in... so to speak. It's very scientific.

GEORGE: Do you mean to say you hand mate these flowers? They're
              not left on their own?

CARETAKER: Yes sir. It's scientific.

GEORGE: You put your fingers in them?

CARETAKER: (He responds in horror) Please, I use a brush, sterilized
              first.

GEORGE: You have destroyed the natural breeding of these roses.

CARETAKER: Here now, we can't have any talk of breeding in the park.
              There are children. Besides, it's called pollinating.

GEORGE: No it isn't. It's called fucking.

CARETAKER: You can't talk like that in the park. It's immoral.

GEORGE: (He shouts at the CARETAKER) You're depriving these roses
              of their sex life. They're being denied free love.

CARETAKER: You're mad.

GEORGE: (He turns to the audience) Ladies and gentlemen, the frost
              is upon us. These pitiful roses which you see before you are
              carriers, advanced scouts of the coming Ice Age. They have
              been deprived of natural love, and can only reach fertiliza-
              tion...

CARETAKER: (He interrupts) Now, enough is enough.

GEORGE: ... by the frosted touch of a scientist's horny brush. But
              this is only the sign of what is to come. A more dangerous
              sign is to be found in our women who, like my wife, have
              placed quiet, secret orders for single beds. And...

CARETAKER: Be quiet, be quiet. I'm not going to have you talking like
              this in my park. Destroying public property. Using profan-
              ity. You're behaving like a mad man. There are children
              playing. Besides, you have to have a licence for public
              assemblage here. So, I think you had best be on your way.
              And don't step on the roses on your way out. It took me
              three weeks to collect the pollen for them.

GEORGE: You flower pervert. Do you know what you do? You rape in-
              nocent flowers. You should be locked up, in an institution
              where you would be unable to lay your obscene hands on help-
              less, virgin roses.

CARETAKER: You've pushed me too far. I'm a patient man, but you better
              move along, before I call the police.
                   (GEORGE does not move, but stands glaring
                    at the CARETAKER)
              I'm warning you. You'd better leave if you don't want to
              be arrested.

GEORGE: Arrested? For what?

CARETAKER: Well, for... for speaking in the park without a licence.

GEORGE: I have a licence.

CARETAKER: You what?

GEORGE: I have a licence, I have my public assemblage licence.

CARETAKER: Well, I think you should leave anyway. Nobody can call me
              a flower pervert in my own park.

GEORGE: You rose-fucker.

CARETAKER: There, you've done it again. Now, you... you just move
              along. I can't stand to be insulted. I'm not a pervert.
              I'm a horticulturist. (He is almost in tears)

GEORGE: You're a communist.

CARETAKER: What?

GEORGE: You're a communist. You're trying to deny my right of
              free speech.

CARETAKER: (He is in tears) I'm a horticulturist!

GEORGE: You're a rose-fucking communist.
                      (GEORGE walks around and picks a rose.
                      He has a smug look on his face. He
                      places the rose in his hair. The CARE-
                      TAKER tries to recover his composure)

CARETAKER: Really, I am a horticulturist. I've never studied it at
              a university, of course, but I've been through the school
              of hard knocks in horticulture. And no one has ever called
              me a rose... those names before.

GEORGE: If you deny me my right of free speech I will do more. I'll
              report you to the police as a traitor to your country.

CARETAKER: Traitor? You can't do it. You were calling me obscene
              names. I never said you couldn't speak. I just told you
              to move a little ways. You could have made your speech
              somewhere else in the park. I never said you couldn't
              speak. Now, did I? Besides, why would you want to give
              a speech anyway? There are no people here. Traitor? Me?
              The authorities would never believe you. Who do you think
              built the park's magnificent flag pole over there? It took
              me twenty years of collecting popsicle sticks in this park
              to build that pole. And I donated all my time, and my own
              private collection of popsicle sticks. It was my part for
              the war effort. So, don't be calling me a traitor.

GEORGE: By chance do you have a speaker's platform?

CARETAKER: We certainly do. I just repainted it. They say it was
              once used by Teddy Roosevelt. Too bad he didn't have a
              chance to see my pole. I know he would have liked it. He
              liked people who had the strength of character to do things
              on their own.

GEORGE: Where is it?

CARETAKER: On the centre of the grounds. You can see it sticking up
              over the tops of the trees.

GEORGE: No, no. I mean the speaker's platform. Where is the
              speaker's platform?

CARETAKER: In storage. It hasn't been used since they dedicated the
              flag pole in 1947. Gave me a medal, they did. The mayor
              himself was there.

GEORGE: I would like to use the stand, if you don't mind.

CARETAKER: You'd what?

GEORGE: I'd like to use the speaker's stand. I have a licence to
             deliver my speech and I wish to exercise my right to use
             the stand. I assume the stand is city property.

CARETAKER: It is, but it's in storage. I just refinished it.

GEORGE: Yes, I know. You told me.

CARETAKER: And you still want to use it?

GEORGE: I do.

CARETAKER: Well, I can't do it now. I have flowers to attend. You
             can't treat hybrids like ordinary flowers. You have to
             look after them all the time. You have to be careful they
             don't become pollinated by some stray bee.

GEORGE: Will you set up the stand?

CARETAKER: Besides, you wouldn't want it today. There won't be any
             people here. This is a working day. Now, if you waited
             until the weekend you could...

GEORGE: Is it, or is it not my constitutional right to use the pub-
             lic speaker's stand?

CARETAKER: It's not a question of rights, it's my roses.

GEORGE: Test-tube babies.

CARETAKER: What?

GEORGE: Test-tube babies. Those roses belong in the Ice Age. They
             have no right to exist. They have no feelings. They're
             just like my wife.

CARETAKER: My roses are hybrids.

GEORGE: Your roses are dead.

CARETAKER: They're so beautiful. I imported the soil.

GEORGE: I don't care to hear the details of how you deprived these
             flowers of sex, just bring me the speaker's stand, and set
             it up over there away from your castrated roses.

CARETAKER: Please stop!

GEORGE: Will you set up the stand?

CARETAKER: I worked thirty-three years...

GEORGE: The stand.

CARETAKER: All right. All right. I'll bring the stand, but there's
not going to be anyone here. And it's a good thing, too
-- with the kind of language you use. (He starts to exit)
He has no right to push me around. A right to speak isn't
a right to insult city employees. I can remember when the
parks were for children.
(He exits. GEORGE looks at his manuscript. He pauses)

GEORGE: Damn smog. I can't see the sun any more. It makes the
world so cold. It makes everything look so murky. The
flowers, the grass, the Caretaker... the roses, and my wife.
And her little murky toy, my daughter. Now there is smog.
Her face is murky even on the days the sun does shine.
She's a by-product of this machine age, this ice-machine
age. Damn dog won't even jump on my lap any more. He just
lays there. Lays there piddling on the rug, and too lazy
to move out of it. And then today those twin beds. It was
the last icicle. My wife brings in those twin beds, and
I knew the end was near. The end of life and the beginning of the Ice Age. (He looks directly at the audience)
This is why, ladies and gentlemen, I have come to you
to sound the warning. Artificially inseminated roses, and
... "You'll sleep better, George Johnson, you'll be fresh-
er for your work" ... the world is coming to an end. Ah
hell, I wonder if it's worth it. Maybe there's too much
to fight. I don't mind the dog so much, but my wife is
different from the dog. At least she tries to walk on two
legs, and makes it... sometimes. Which is why I have
come to speak to you today about man as a free agent.
(The CARETAKER enters dragging the
speaker's platform)

CARETAKER: I told you there wasn't going to be a crowd. It's a waste
of time.

GEORGE: All of life is a waste of time.

CARETAKER: It doesn't seem to me you're accomplishing anything if
you're speaking and there isn't anyone listening.

GEORGE: I don't care if anyone ever listens.

CARETAKER: I've never heard of anything so silly. You don't care if
anyone listens? What do you need the speaker's stand for
then?

GEORGE: I don't know. It seems right to have it.

CARETAKER: Why not try this weekend. You'd pack them in. People around here haven't seen an exciting public speech since the radicals who sprang up during the Depression. Come on the weekend and try it.

GEORGE: No, I think I have to do it now. It's like that, you know. (The CARETAKER nods) I'm sorry I was so harsh with you. I guess I'm a little worked up.

CARETAKER: Oh, it's all right. I know how you feel. It was the same way with me and the popsicle sticks. It was something I had to do. I couldn't really tell you why. People used to say I was crazy. It's just for years I had been picking up those sticks and throwing them in the trash, and it seemed to be such a waste of nature's lumber. So I decided to make them useful. It's a lovely piece of work, my flag pole. You should see it when you're finished.

GEORGE: I will, I promise you.

CARETAKER: Of course, now it's flowers with me. There's something nice about helping them grow. My wife never much liked them though. It's been fun having this job in the park. Thirty-three years next August.

GEORGE: Your wife doesn't like flowers?

CARETAKER: It was the bugs that bothered her. I used to spray them but it never seemed to help. Well, there's your platform. I wish it were a better day for it. People don't do any speaking nowadays. There should be more of it.

GEORGE: Perhaps, I really don't know. I haven't done much of this myself. It's just my wife, and now my daughter.

CARETAKER: This is a strange topic. Nothing like it in the Great Depression.

GEORGE: Life is so murky. I had no intention of making a speech, but those damn twin beds...

CARETAKER: It's the smog, makes everything murky. Probably what stopped the bees. They can't tell when it's spring any more. That's why I work on the roses.

GEORGE: It seems like such a terrible waste that flowers have lost their incentive. It seems a little more understandable with people. My mother had fourteen children. My wife had one.

GEORGE: (Cont'd) She complained for three months afterwards about the pain and said it kept her from looking nice for me. I've felt ashamed ever since. Ashamed for having the damn kid.

CARETAKER: How terrible. A man shouldn't have to feel that way.

GEORGE: I know. I tried to tell my wife, but...

CARETAKER: Did you ever think of taking up horticulture? It's a great help for passing the time and working off tensions.

GEORGE: Is that why you're... Is your wife cold too?

CARETAKER: She is cold all right. She's been dead for five years.

GEORGE: I'm sorry... I didn't...

CARETAKER: It's all right. I'm not bothered by her death. It was her time. Besides, we gave her a fine funeral. Took the procession right past the flag pole. She would have liked it. She used to say it was the only worthwhile thing I ever did. I gave her a big wreath of my roses, too. And two years ago, I took some of the soil off her grave and mixed it into my flower beds, so you might say she is still with me, in the roses.

GEORGE: What a lovely funeral. You must have been very close.

CARETAKER: No, not really. When I stop to think about her I guess she was what you might call cold. But I never really thought about it much. I've always had the gardening.

GEORGE: Your wife was frigid?

CARETAKER: Well, she was always shy. From the time I married her. She used to think men were ugly, and I guess they are.

GEORGE: Did you have twin beds?

CARETAKER: Oh yes, she bought them wholesale from her uncle. He was...

GEORGE: Twin beds.

CARETAKER: ... a furniture salesman.

GEORGE: Damn. I knew it. I knew I was right. Everyone. Everyone caught in this refrigerated atmosphere is buying twin beds.

CARETAKER: It's the atomic bomb testing.

GEORGE: What?

CARETAKER: The atomic bombs. They're ruining the atmosphere. Awfully hard on the plants.

GEORGE: Yes, the plants. They're even using separate beds now.

CARETAKER: Well, you can't put them all in one bed, it would choke their roots.

GEORGE: And you're providing them!

CARETAKER: I'm what?

GEORGE: You're providing the twin beds and stifling any sexual in-itiative.

CARETAKER: It's the bomb.

GEORGE: (He becomes upset again) There's no feeling in it. Every-one lays around waiting for others to produce. Like your damn roses. They should have the energy to do their own fucking.
       (GEORGE'S wife, DOROTHY, and his DAUGHTER
       enter the stage. They stand to one side
       and are quiet and extremely controlled
       throughout the play. They are not seen
       by GEORGE or the CARETAKER at this point)

CARETAKER: Say now, listen, you're becoming upset again. I think you better relax before you offend someone. You wouldn't want to hurt anyone, would you?

GEORGE: All i ever am is worked up. There's too much relaxing in this world. You should see my wife. Now, there's a woman who knows how to relax. When she lies in bed she can spread herself out like molasses, and climbing on top of her can offer about the same experience. Someone, for God's sake, has to become worked up. If everyone...

CARETAKER: Now, I'm sorry but you'll have to stop. I've enjoyed our little talk and all, but you can't be carrying on like this in the park, even if you do have a licence.

GEORGE: Don't you understand I'm trying to save you?

DOROTHY: (She walks over to her husband) George. George? Will you come home now?

GEORGE: (He is surprised) What?

DOROTHY: If you're finished with your speech, we would like for you
            to come home. We've been holding dinner for you.

GEORGE: Why... why are you here? Did you hear what I was saying?
            How long have you been here?

DOROTHY: We know you missed work today, but it's all right, you've
            been under a heavy strain. But you shouldn't miss dinner.
            I think you should finish your speech and come home.

GEORGE: I will not. I have eight pages to go.

DOROTHY: But you'll miss dinner, and I've mashed the potatoes for you.

GEORGE: Damn your potatoes. Didn't you hear what I've been saying?

CARETAKER: Is this your wife? I'd look out if I were you, you've been
            saying some...

GEORGE: How long have you been here?

DOROTHY: With the special gravy you always liked.

GEORGE: Can't you hear me? I hate your damn dinners.

CARETAKER: You mustn't mind him, ma'am. I don't think he's really
            angry with you. He's a little worked up over the roses.
            He claims I've been fu... messing around with them. I
            think if you took him home he'd be all right.

DOROTHY: George doesn't like roses. Do you, George? They're bad
            for your asthma.

GEORGE: Don't like roses! I love roses! I've never had asthma and
            I think they're the only life left with any feelings. Ex-
            cept when you put them in separate beds... like this pervert.

CARETAKER: I've told you not to insult me.

DOROTHY: We can see the roses after dinner.

GEORGE: Dorothy, can't you understand me? I don't like these
            roses.

CARETAKER: Speaking for my roses, I'm sure the feeling is mutual.

DOROTHY: I've ordered an orthopedic mattress for you, the Henry the
            VIII type. It will help your hernia.

GEORGE: There you go again. Trying to destroy me. Everyone we meet,
            you have to tell them about my hernia.

DOROTHY: Well, you do have one. But I don't want to offend you.

CARETAKER: You'd be smart to listen to your wife and move along home.
             With a hernia it's not good to get worked up and strain
             yourself.

GEORGE: Damn my hernia. Go home with my wife? You go home with her.
             Or better yet, let her go home with Henry the VIII, she's
             got his beds. (Speaks to his wife) Would you like that?
             Maybe he would behead you. Wouldn't it be nice. You'd be
             right at home. You could munch on an apple and not feel
             a thing. You could tell him when it's over, "Do you feel
             better now dear?" You could lay there and ooze all over
             the bed like you always do.

DOROTHY: Marcia misses her daddy. Don't you, Marcia?
                 (The CHILD, aged about seven, who has
                  been watching with interest, nods yes)
             Tell daddy how much you miss him, Marcia.

GEORGE: Keep your brat away from me, she's diseased.

CARETAKER: You're talking to your daughter!

GEORGE: She's my wife's daughter.

DOROTHY: You're daddy's little baby, aren't you, Marcia.
                 (MARCIA nods yes)

CARETAKER: I think you're a maniac. You're a sick man. You shouldn't
             insult your wife and daughter.

GEORGE: Why not? They can't feel it.

CARETAKER: Everyone has feelings.

GEORGE: Everyone used to have feelings... before the Ice Age.

CARETAKER: (Speaks to DOROTHY) Perhaps you should call the police.

DOROTHY: Daddy's just tired. Aren't you, daddy?

GEORGE: No. I'm not tired. I feel fine. Don't tell me how I feel.
             You don't know. You don't know anything, and I'm not com-
             ing home. Ever! Do you hear me?

DOROTHY: The mashed potatoes will become cold.

GEORGE: Do you know what I've been saying about you to this per-
             vert here? I'm been telling him you are a frigid bitch.
             A frigid bitch. Now will you leave me alone?

DOROTHY: You've always liked your potatoes mashed. Mommy's little helper mashed them herself. Didn't you, Marcia?
    (MARICA nods yes)

GEORGE: I told him you have an icebox between your legs. You're a meat freezer. (He speaks to the CARETAKER) Look at her. She won't even react. She's as dead as your pitiful roses.

CARETAKER: I'd react if you were saying those things about me. I'd do more. I'd be mad. I'd be damn mad. (Speaks to DOROTHY) You go ahead, ma'am. Go ahead and let him have it. He deserves it.

DOROTHY: George is irritated because he's tired and hungry.

CARETAKER: You can't let him say those things. He was insulting you.

GEORGE: Go ahead, Dorothy. Blast me. Let me have it. Give it to me, just once. (Speaks to the CARETAKER) There. You see, she can't do it. She can't feel anything.

CARETAKER: Well, if she doesn't, I do. I can't stand by and watch a man treat his wife in such a disgusting manner. It isn't proper.

GEORGE: What about the way she treats me? Can't you see what's happening?

CARETAKER: I can see all right. I can see when it's time for me to teach a man a little respect for women and children. I may be old, but I'm not too old to square off with you.
    (The CARETAKER takes off his jacket
    and begins to roll up his sleeves.
    Then ne stops)
What am I doing? I can't be mixed up in this. I'll lose my job.

DOROTHY: Quit upsetting the man, George. Will you come home?

GEORGE: Shut up, you bitch. (He speaks to the CARETAKER) She can't win. She can't win now. You have something left. You almost lost your temper. Did you feel it? Did you feel what was happening?

CARETAKER: Leave me alone. It's none of my business.

GEORGE: Don't stop now. Give it a chance. Do something. Throw me out of the park. Throw them out of the park. Help me with my speech. We'll wait for the crowds on the weekend. Destroy the roses.

CARETAKER: No! Are you out of your mind? I couldn't do it. I love my roses. Stay away from me. Thirty-three years I've worked on these roses.

GEORGE: Don't you understand? I'm trying to save you. Doesn't anyone understand me?

DOROTHY: Of course we understand. You're tired and hungry and upset. Come home and have something to eat. Then you'll feel better.

GEORGE: Will you leave me alone. I'm trying to talk...

CARETAKER: I don't want to talk. Just go away. Leave me alone. I was happy before you came.

DOROTHY: After dinner you can try your new bed.

GEORGE: I'm not interested in the bed.

DOROTHY: You have to try it sometime.

GEORGE: Can I try yours?

DOROTHY: What about your hernia? You have the orthopedic mattress.

GEORGE: Do you see? It isn't our bed. It's his and hers and Henry the VIIIth's.

CARETAKER: Go home. Will you please go home and leave me alone? You've made me feel funny. I don't like to feel this way. Just go. You're breaking up your family.

GEORGE: There is no family. My family is as dead as your roses.

DOROTHY: Come home, George.

CARETAKER: My roses aren't dead.

GEORGE: They won't breed.

DOROTHY: It's dinner time.

CARETAKER: But, they're hybrids.

GEORGE: So's my wife.

DOROTHY: The twin beds are here, George.

GEORGE: <u>You are dead!</u>

CARETAKER: But your daughter. You can at least think of her. You have to go home for your daughter. You could at least keep her from...

GEORGE: No! I won't go back.

DOROTHY: Marcia wants daddy to hold her hand while she's crossing the busy street. Don't you, Marcia?
(MARCIA nods yes)

CARETAKER: She's your own flesh and blood. You have to help her.

GEORGE: It's too late. It's too damn late. The bees have stopped, and there's too much smog and hate.

DOROTHY: (Speaks to MARCIA) Take daddy's hand. Daddy will take us home.

GEORGE: Don't you ever listen? I'm not going. You're a frigid bitch and my daughter is dead. (Speaks to the CARETAKER) Help me.

CARETAKER: Maybe you'd better leave him, ma'am. Sell the twin beds. There's really something nice about a man and a woman on one large bed.

DOROTHY: Take daddy's hand, Marcia.

GEORGE: Keep your brat away from me.
(MARCIA comes closer and closer to GEORGE, who keeps backing away like a frightened animal)
Keep her away. I don't want to touch your damned machine.

DOROTHY: Take his hand.

GEORGE: No!
(MARCIA has reached GEORGE by this time. GEORGE, in his emotional frenzy, strikes his daughter. The CHILD stands motionless. She does not react)
(Softly) I'm sorry. I'm so sorry. I didn't mean it. Don't cry. I didn't mean to hurt you. You won't hate me, will you?
(GEORGE moves closer to his daughter and looks into her face. The CHILD does not react)
Oh my God, she's not crying. She won't even cry.

DOROTHY: What a brave strong girl.

GEORGE: She can't even cry. There's too much smog in the air. It's
             killing the roses.

DOROTHY: Will daddy come home with us now?
                  (DOROTHY picks up the CHILD'S hand and
                  places it in GEORGE'S hand. They begin
                  to lead GEOURGE off)

CARETAKER: (Screams out) No! No! Don't go home with them!

GEORGE: (He speaks to the CARETAKER) I thought all children cried.

CARETAKER: They do. I know. I've heard them.

GEORGE: There won't be any roses before long. They'll all be dead.

DOROTHY: The beds are made of walnut. I know you'll like them.
             They're coloured like the flag pole over there.
                  (They exit. The CARETAKER stares after them)

THE END